T0162431

THE PRESENTABLE ART OF READING ABSENCE

THE PRESENTABLE ART OF READING ABSENCE

Jay Wright

DALKEY ARCHIVE PRESS CHAMPAIGN AND LONDON

Library of Congress
Cataloging-in-Publication Data
Wright, Jay, 1934–
The presentable art of reading absence / Jay Wright. — 1st ed.
p. cm.
ISBN-13: 978-1-56478-498-8 (acid-free paper)
ISBN-10: 1-56478-498-3 (acid-free paper)
I. Title.
PS3573.R5364P74 2008
811'.54—dc22
2007042157

Partially funded by a grant from the Illinois
Arts Council, a state agency, and by the
University of Illinois, Urbana-Champaign

www.dalkeyarchive.com

Designed and composed by Quemadura
Printed on permanent/durable
acid-free, recycled paper, and bound
in the United States of America

THE PRESENTABLE ART OF READING ABSENCE

Here begins the revelation of a kiosk
beside the road: the white eggs
nestled there in straw
turn blue in the amber light.
Make of that what you will,
          say, what you desire,
a pilgrimage,
          a secular mourning,
a morning given over to meditation.
This is the place set aside
     for creating the body,
a source of fluctuations, unmarked
                    by singularity.
Call this wandering along this road
a colonization.

Somos ese quimérico museo de formas
                    inconstantes,

"In the duration of time ..."
But that, along this road,
                    is the question,
a movement beyond anxiety.

Read again that archaeological sentence,
that syntax that determines a cursus planus.

Now through the metonymic night
            I knew
                the scuppered scansion,
and behind the name (Borges I name you)
lay the blue needle of namelessness,
but one must not insist on the musicality
                                of terms.
So must I inscribe the dog star
                    just there,
just where
sentences sound a diminished seventh,
though a raised sixth had been a possible
emplotment.
                Let's get on with it
and, yes, getting on with it is the point.

This room is as close as you will get to sorrow.
Not half the ransom in brown robes,
      or the star configuration of the choir,
            the wedged bed in the rancid stall,
                  the mewling intent of a winter's wind
belongs,
      shapes,
drives the melancholic astral brush
along the parsimonious river—
                  the river, the room,
an abandoned music that cleverly returns.
This room is only a brown space,
the habitation and tomb
            of the lourie bird.
Take that down through the meadow,
from which, at the most distant point,
a bell sounds
      and someone is singing,
or it might be partridge
            thrashing the late grass.
These accounts
sustain the morning's silence,

and initiate a festivity
         that seems forever out of place.
This instant
becomes the smallest unit of meaning
in the universe,
         an aberration
that clarifies our contingency.
         One learns to speak
         of solar viscera,
         or of the chemical conception
                  of perception—
         scarifications upon the face of existence.

This house remains scarred
by the non-initiate's entry; mark
         the incisions that sit on slippered sills,
the surgical protrusion by the doorlock.
Why have we come
to a habitation so violated by deception
and ambition?
                  Nothing invites
the silence we require. But that is now

to enter again, having given
an account that molds an ancient
                    silence in place.
How small our being,
how insignificant our flagellant
movement toward fulfillment, toward
                    an arrested light.

What do you bring to the door?
            A Sonoran mud turtle
            the red clay that surrounds Jemez
            a banana leaf from a grove in Córdoba

A foghorn on the coastal dawn
elicits a train ride through a desert valley.
The withered parchment of a perfect April
begins the sonic insistence of a spirit
                    on the wing.
There will be nothing as tangible as death
when the pulse escapes.
                Someone
must go forward with the proper measure.

There, as I speak,
the injured spirit forgets

                its instruction.

Who will notice
the clamor of a bare foot upon a bare floor,
or the day's silver sheen of a moon

        that refuses to disappear?

Who will be attentive
to the edge and bite of barberry,
or the geometrical relation

        of bloodroot and ivy?

I must not think of that trilling owl,
or the sharp-noted stream as it passes;

           I must not think.

I sit in error,
or so would I stand,
confused by the metrical command

        of my breath,

breath-weary with the meter of a dry cell body,
and there proceed to an intimation

        of measure.

Suppose now
the exception of the light
that comes with the cardinal's disappearance.
Surely,
someone will say we can begin
deep in that uninhabited mass,
or start again, and once again,
burdened by our delight
            in corrupt symmetry.
There must be an inelastic
attention to this moment,
            or this flagged instant
so harmoniously disposed
in the red body of doubt
            that has suddenly appeared.
Call it true measure,
or a parity of souls too familiar
            to be attentive.

What do you leave at the door?
A bowl of green chile
the bluest flower of Zapopan
a goshawk's exhilarated cry

We begin with a possible misconception:
an electron that turns upon itself.
That physicist has abandoned us
    here
        where a radiant force
            steps up, steps down—
a troubled prehensive act.
This morning
I covet a troubled necessity.
I step up and step down
    a scalar plethora of mind,
and find myself distended,
            undefined.
Simple words exhilarate us,
a simple motive stretches the spine.
We pretend a techné of movement,
a complicity with a transformative,
            turbulent moment.
Such is peace,
and such the motive and lie,
and we have not yet arrived.
    One must learn not to pray.

One must learn to release the sunlight
and to allow a magnetic dissonance
            in a bird voice that enters the ear.
Nothing here
needs the evidence of that photon
perched on the sill of the square window
            at the end of the room,
or the symmetry of its resemblance
to any silver spark of dust.
I resume:
            such is peace,
and such is the inexact profession
of a pilgrim proceeding
            toward the point of his own
                        erasure.
I awaken to a fraudulent tribute,
a memorial
            I wouldn't wish upon
an abandoned crow.
                        Such doxa
and mimetic desire can only teach
the art of dissimulation.

I turn again,
counting, one breath
one and one,
trying to elicit a stability
in movement,
an uneasiness in being still.
Within the graveyard,
the wind has taken hold.
As you advance,
you realize the incongruous chestnuts
have been cut by the wind,
and scattered about the gravestones.
Ask yourself now,
should winter be an appropriate
response to this moment,
or a fig tree rise from a memory
of Zempoala?
When did you come through the door?
You notice the silver, faceless platter
that has nothing to do
with the state of that
confusion of birds.

Leave that.
Release
the dark lace of light
that grips this room.
                "An image insists . . ."
                        Such an argument
obscures the memorial's intent.
You are learning
to move from circle to circle,
without moving,
                riding, without body,
upon transfigured breath.
                So you would say
that once an ivory figure spun
its invitation
to its miraculous beheading—
                a parlor game you must not
                                recall.
This body feels chambered by all
that has escaped
a constellation of intent,
only, perhaps,

the brightest intent of a star,
a piping fish, endangered
                    by troubled air.
From breath to breath,
the world is disfigured,
                    reconstructed,
                              let go.

(The lights reveal the epitome of a wash, with yucca elata sit-
ting sternly in place. A small man, wearing a white guayabera
and white cotton trousers, swerves in an irresolute light. His
hair shines in its darkness. His skin, in the exposed face and
bare feet, displays the leathery flexibility of the yucca leaf. The
man kneels, scoops the warm air from the ground to bathe
his face. A black panel slides over this scene, removes it. An
auburn-haired woman, wearing a coarse brown cotton robe,
cinched by a yellow belt, appears. She carries a large, traylike
basket on her left hip. Her bare feet grip the ground. A white
panel slides over this scene, removes it. A bay horse slouches
toward an isolated adobe wall. A garrulous moon announces
the deepest midnight or the jubilation of the coldest dawn.
Silence is a shawl of blue-tinged white. No screen arrives.)

The henna-haired ocotillo
the sweet-scented heliotrope
the four-wing saltbush
winter fat

    all things
    out-of-place
    out-of-time

Would that I had my deepest midnight,
a winter perhaps out of phase,
the consolation of the laser line of Aries,
the misconception that awakens
    this conceptual dawn.
Would that desire would walk away.
    Who will take me in hand,
if not the insufferable one,
objectified by suffering?

    Whole and everywhere mark
    this objectification
of an unseizable compassion
and the ingenuity
    of a heliostat of passion.

Why now defend
the labyrinth that defines
every intentional bereavement,
at the beginning,
                    a shading
into an intensional end?
Remove nothing.
Replace emptiness.

This narrow road leads to a dry hour
and the paradox of an attentive body.
Each instant reconfigures its death.
One must sit still.
One must sit straight.
The light that strays through the fraying oak
must be the exact
                    measure of its own absence.
We could go up to the top of the hill,
and restructure our entrance,
                    do away
with the contradiction of being
nowhere but here,

the assumed proportion of a presence
that will always escape,
of being nowhere

                  but near
the presumed indifference
that solicits our wakefulness.
Day begins
its indiscreet translation

                  once again,
flowing through the pearl white of loss,
or the indelible deep blue

                  of fractured words.
Remove emptiness.
Replace nothing.

I will place my thought
at the top of that tree, and move
against my familiar direction, beyond
the scalar indifference my body

                  requires.
Where does the inelastic collision begin?
Where is the flaw, if not in the mind,

if not in the resonant body of a word
that binds us in its limits?
Let us ignore the bird's name,
and be attentive to the triple-tonguing
flare of its song,
to the fact of its assault upon
the box-elder, dying at the yard's edge.
Surely,
some clarification will arise
with the brute sensation of movement.
Or will stillness robe us
against the coldness our insecurity

                  unveils?
The sound
the peasant brook engenders

          warms the room.
I call this a Monday in March.
Out of the lilac temper of summer,
the rose-breasted grosbeak accuses me of error.
Did I, in the past,
sit at this spot, with my mind fixed

         on the arrival of light?

I repeat   I cannot   I do not
            count the breath
                    as ancient as the thought
The convulsive propulsion of grace
might awaken me.
                    I might be taken
once again through the geometry
of a perfect misapprehension,
the linear relation of nothingness
                    and joy,
the spatial dimension of emptiness
                    and resignation.
The design fails;
            the voice says we must whisper
                    an unimpeachable word,
which will not take its place
on a Monday in March.
Perhaps it would be better
to establish the song of the ruddy duck,
or to seek the metrical
                    assistance and embryonic
necessity of the red-breasted merganser,

phrasing its passion

                      out of phase

with winter's predictable closure.

My passion now is improvised,

momentary, changeable.

I would embrace

that indeterminate rise and fall,

that inarticulate, unmeasured sound

                  of a letter witlessly shaped,

a fashion of continuity passion

                      will not allow,

not a matter fixed by Fassungskraft,

or a text of endurable compassion.

March is a matter of April,

or so we propose it,

a just proportion, expressively bland,

              or blind, as the case may be.

That phrase is inexact.

The world does not submit

to the spontaneous joy that has run

aground in search of its measure.

April is a matter of June,
a process of metrical ambiguity.
Now,
outside, through the window,
we see green things appear.
Someone says that we have been blind.
Someone begins a relevant narrative.
Gradually, I awaken.
I select the most pertinent movements
of the day before me,
the thetic and arsic beats that promise
a congenial rhythm.

                I pretend,
overriding the depth of doubt,
that silence has become my tunable bell,
an impulse that discharges
                my virtuous ambition.
Someone has said,
            congratulations, you know
            the hour of your death.
And so I do.
And so I have died twice,

and again,
a creature of hidden streams
that spell salvation upon my body's
        faithful and abraded text.
What makes this strict benevolence
appeal to me?
                This flagellant mind
will argue with itself and fall swiftly
toward its own beginning, there
where the flight of a winter wren
                obscures my shadow.

If, now, the bell rings,
who will respond? I have placed
myself in the way of my own
                displacement.
Start again.
The clock is in the bowl of rice.
A grain of dust has become
        a measure of eternity.
The voice of a ravished hare
assaults the stillness.

The chattering tin on the barn roof
borrows the wind's voice.
The timid sound lodged in a hen's throat
speaks of a danger no one can face.
Start again.
With the Eye of God on the far wall
With the iron insistence of the Edan Ogboni
           lying placidly on an Indian cloth
With the silent syntax of the Dogon doorlock
                              in that corner
With the floor's intemperate warmth
under bare feet
              Who can respond?
              Who is in attendance?

But there again,
someone has died, or the body
has reconfigured a space forever denied.

Orgullo, dicen.
I heard you speak of passion
as though you were patron of fire.

Notice how metaphor escapes,
and how every discrimination
                    runs into a perfect
                              darkness,
or a silence.
                    Never mind.
And never a mind,
or the instant apprehension of what
is passing, or to come.
Does time reside in the body of your teacher,
or in the extravagant words
          he gives you license to say?
You catch the flaw.
What is the proper form of that body?

That body is as inconceivable
as the bead ticking of desert rain,
or the meandering intelligence
          that would adorn a dying river.
One hears the liquid root
of such expectation;
                    one can,

as the loveliest of men did,
speak of memory.
                    Think of it,
and give in to that resident feeling,
rain falling upon a valley
that no longer belongs to you,
a gift of an inexplicable compassion—
something unspeakable
                    flowing
over the mind's rocky barrier,
                    marking
the water's benevolent flow.
                    Some say my compadre
carried this low Latin beyond sense,
fell fatefully in love
with turbid, torrential, glacial streams,
with the unbidden blood coursing
                    in shallow outlets.
Who is to say
what absence matters,
when the letter that defines a river bank
                    disappears?

Let me call them now,
fresh out of this estranged morning,
for the comfort of the soul we buried:

> Ajijic
>
> Chapala
>
> the Rhone
>
> the Nile
>
> the Mississippi

and let us sit now
before a simple meal,

> a tamale in a banana leaf,
>
> a dish of the sweetest plantains,
>
> an assortment of *pan,*
>
> the darkest bean-filled coffee —

almost such an offering
as upon the Day of the Dead,

> almost the inverse formation
>
> > of solitude.

How the blue of this absent water prevails.
Small rivers, such as this,
turn upon themselves, and begin
the tolling of the sacraments,

that first beat in the mind's dance,

in the spirit's indeterminate permutations.

Anámnesis,

a village gift the water borrows.

The sun shivers the glass

into sound,

the faint note of a distant bird.

The master has placed his robe

upon a rock at the base of the Nile.

The narrative dissolves

              to allow my teacher

to speak of God's memory,

and of that triple being within the self.

He will, will he not?,

ask me to avoid my own incarnation.

But the face is mine.

The sacrament remains corrupt.

No image

      sustains;

           nothing

               speaks of unfolding.

The master went to London incognito,
or, that is to say,
he was incognito in London,
or London had arrived incognito.
The distinction deserves as much regard
as that between memory and anámnesis.
                    I strike my irọ́kẹ́.
                              At this rate,
love will go down as
the fear of divination,
or the source of continuity
                    within divinity.
Search that mensural determinacy
for the law that breeds expectation.

The blue spruce,
with its clerical prosody,
shames me again into silence.
What so engages as the thoroughly
broken rhythm,
                    that momentary
fiction,

an infinite density
that pulses as music demands
when the body flows
out of its previous age,
released from its binding impulse,
its absolute rest?
I would ask that burning February morning
to return—
as once in agonistic
intuition my spirit moved aimlessly
through death's invitation.
Nothing should encourage this singing
in my bones, this sign
and devastation that always waits
in lengthening shadows.
I cannot know not
feel not see not
with what will not
arise in the necessary texture
that frees me from my arrested breath.
My grief is a resolution
I have dedicated to the exhilaration

that sustain's faith's
                bitter almond.
Why now speak of faith?
Sit here,
facing the blank wall
of an unimaginable universe,
the inventive deceit that tells me
                that love is dead,
or unspeakable,
a possible disguise that leads
to imperfection and a blessing.
This morning chases a scattered rhyme;
this moment flows toward its ambivalent source.
I know, but will not insist,
that there is an "epitome of Gods great booke
                        of creatures,"
and one who goes disguised
                as il miglior fabbro.
Dream now of Argentina,
        and know it is a violation
                of this movement,
one that compassion has led us

                              to start,

                     such tinctures

                     and Trinities

                              lying displaced,

all human by the face of analogy

     restless   breathless   continent

                              unbearably desirable.

North by northwest,

I am but blind and sullen

with praise,

                     my mind

a sleeping or a fervent bee.

Is there a rule

for the light that slopes

from the troposphere to a sightless eye?

Such clever words

that speak of disapproval,

syllables torn from their consenting

frame,

the mind settling here

for the long ride into disdain.

But since I' am dead, and buried, I could frame

          no epitaph, which might advance . . .

Dream of the island
my voice has made of my fame,
the debilitating temper of poor songs
that testify.
Why uncover a perfect sacrifice
that leads only to a grave of one's
own thoughts,
a punning excuse for abandoning
a great feast,
having no grace to say?
I am not then from Court.

To know and to feele all this,
to make my distemper
part of the bindery of my spirit
and at once the measure of this
radiant moment
structures a deceptive absence.

So you will listen,
in the ordained silence,
for a syncopation you have not heard before.
So you will mark,
with your eye's rhythm,

the limits of your concern and competence
in the structuring emptiness.

For thirty minutes,
this body has lifted an indefinable weight.

To know and to feele all this, and not
to have Words, and to pursue
no affirmation—the mind
a sleeping or a fervent bee,
perhaps a Rhine-based artificer,
blinded by a Florentian luxury.
Leave me here,
where no thing is,
where the patience for purity wounds.

... y con algún remordimiento
de mi complicidad en el resurgimiento del día,
I go under a simple case
or above an adiabatic moment
in the fields,
feeling la noche gastada,

sure of my anointment
　　　　through the salutary
dimension of old songs.
　　　　I shall call it
an Hibernian law, a postulate
that keeps me moving toward a
　　　　　　contradiction.
I go under an extravagant supposition.
I awaken to my soul's entropy.
Can the bear hide in the quaking aspen?
Can the quaking aspen hide the bear?
I must guard against
this pickpocket precedent, this
fire and fasting that lead
　　　　away from this clarified instant.
I must be less attentive
to the black shawl my lover misplaced
　　　　　　in Cartagena,
or attentive, nevertheless,
　　　　to the placement of Cartagena,
all fire and liberal dicing,
　　　　an embellishment of loss.

That singer no longer belongs
near the banyan tree;
that singer no longer belongs
to me.

           Start again with the music's count.
A black bear dancing in the aspens
declares the forest's figurative intent.
What could a Florentine disgest
in a pun,
a dun and able configuration
of satyres,

             drawing my envy,

                   perhaps my contempt?
Content with the swelling
assessment of fraternity, my mind

                settles into its

                treacherous orbit.
So had your body 'her morning,
given in the incompatible dreams
      of that other pilgrim.
There is an hour
when the pilgrim lifts

the morning's liberating cup
           on Corrientes,
and the muezzin depth of the tango
disrupts his contemplation,
and the green lorquiano intensity
           again becomes bearable.
Outside,
todo en el aire es pájaro,
not the shell of a woman
           lacing wheat in a sun-benumbed field.
The day will pass,
or come undone at the edge of the water,
where the boats stand in the bronze of evening,
and we might cross a shallow channel
into another city's peace.
                Who goes there,
where all is memory and resignation,
and the streets seem miscast
with names that once wore the sporran
                respect
peculiar to an island
           we had abandoned?

It would therefore be advisable
to consider a ladybug upon a rock
and the desert emptiness that illuminates
its small mask,
           all things in debt
to an egregious error,
a continuity, a fossil pace,
           the borrowed syntax.

The dancer turns
toward an electric blue aurora,
the magnetic flow.
           Whose footprints are these?
No one has an answer
to the spinning exigencies of dust,
or to the contest I have established
as I sit, divesting myself of dream.
           This body, on this chair,
feels the eruption of its cunning,
the gathering of its own constraints.
One and one and also
    meditation   remembrance   and song

the indigenous articulation of moments
                    always in flight.
I will not despair.
I have learned that even
prominences can erupt, can escape.
What gets done on the castle stairs
might resonate in Buenos Aires,
        or become a desperate correction
to Granada's wizened deadness
or the London locutionary grave
or the quaint planetary inception in Florence.
Yet someone, in my name,
has written upon the forest
                    in white and black and red.
But, oh, there is a singing
in this abandoned temple;
tell such singing of abandonment.
The white clothes,
            given to my resurrection,
lie soiled by forgetfulness,
forgetful now,
in themselves, of the instruments

that gave them life,

               the charted

history of my supplicant's voice,

the knife and cowry shell of pen

                  and parchment.

Slowly,

these daedalian scribes

gather for their custom—

         the singular, salutary, timeless text

         I will not do, but do

         a perfect sacrifice,

               and will burn it.

They have me at the gathering,

a celebration of intent,

an improbable resolution

        their cunning calls into being.

My song might be a leather belt

adorned with precious stones,

or a cloud of dust and gas, swirling

through my body's tempered execution.

I am learning the obligatory

suppression of various signs, the default

and defect in affective moments.
And where does the body go,
                    when I transmute my name?

I live on the edge of acceptance
and desire,
                    knowing I am in error,
and have been instructed by those
who had read the past and knew
                    that grace would fail me.
Sitting with folded hands,
I have become devious, a danger
to my own engagement.
                              My body
marks the hours,
                    as they flow
into substance and incongruity.
My mind
trumpets its earned exhilaration.
I wait here
to lay this text upon such altars
as prize my devotion.

Devotion
        has become the other side
              of being.
Should I become a specular stone,
'transparent as glasse, or crystall'?
Pity the curandero his mesa,
his power an altar, set with glass,
shells, a rattle, holy water—
        all a compensation
for the evasive sentence,
for the silence structuring an absolute
                past.
¿Cuando estaré tranquilo / del abandono
del amigo?
The canon danced
under the sound of my voice,
yet I knew myself embraced
        by his evensong.
We sat in the darkness,
commemorating the virgin,
self-gravitating systems spinning
        out of balance.

I am speaking to you now.
Surely, we have arrived.

      This is an infallible claim:
to sit in this garden and to know it,
to watch the evasive sun play
over the juniper,

              and to feel the absent
hemlock breathing in the distance,
and to covet the astonishment of astilbe
embellishing a hidden path.
So the two of us sit,
mov'd with reverentiall anger,

           no longer at rest.
This must be the moment of separation,
the first betrayal,
the first ferrying of a constellation
that reminds me that stars

    form in the ash of other stars

        as they approach their end.
I would betray this ontological event;
I would trace my birth on water,
in the turbulence of a nurturing faith.

I say my star is nearest earth,

and that my light is mortal.

These sojourners,

these clarions of mid-May,

twins of the deep song,

given substance in spiritual desire,

step diffidently into the garden.

I say Thou seest me here at midnight,

searching the other side of life.

This is the story of the little boats.

(Two small boats, each with a solitary figure standing erect within it, progress through a rapidly flowing basin. The figures gradually reveal themselves to be women—one robed in white, one robed in red. The boat on the left, looking east, appears to be pursuing the boat on the right, as they head west. A third boat appears, fit for but showing no sail, as the others do, and carrying a woman robed in black. This boat moves east, and confronts the second boat. The woman speaks, "Do you know that she is pursuing you?" The second woman answers, "But I am pursuing her." "That," the woman of the black robe responds, "seems incongruous at least and absurd on the face of it. I must come aboard, and make sure of your rationality." The woman in the red robe turns, and steers away to the east. The woman in white and the woman in black now face each other. The black-robed woman speaks, "Do you know that she is pursuing you?" "That," the woman of the white robe responds, "is incongruous at least and absurd on the face of it. I must come aboard and make sure of your reason." The boat carrying the woman in black veers off course, and reappears on the left, following the woman in red. The woman of the white robe speaks to herself, "I follow my own constellation. No one can say I am out of my hemisphere. I am as bright as any sun. I shine where I shine." She veers away, and turns up on the left following the black-robed woman. The woman in red speaks to herself, "No one can match my dance of delight. Silly minnesingers confuse my joy with measure." She cuts away, reappears on the left, following the woman in white. The woman in black speaks to herself, "Should I attend to the water flowing here? Should I hide for a moment? Will the light follow me?" She moves away, comes up on the left following the woman in red. The three boats weave, rapidly changing places, at times becoming entangled with each other. They end, lying parallel to each other in the order black, white and red, all facing in the same direction. The women stand in the boats, and raise their arms in supplication. Their mouths open and shut; no words come.)

/mi corazón es una ofrenda y mis lágrimas
  son piedras rituales

Where now should I put the question
of suffering,
                  these broken statues in Mérida,
the gypsy veil for a Spanish saint?
Down this solitary road,
I have appealed to my blindness.
Deigne at my hands this crown of prayer
                                    and praise.
I feel the rhythm of an inescapable
liberation. Nothing will save me.
          Nothing can possibly
lift the weight of my meditation
and send me scurrying
into the unexamined dark,

into the flow of another life.
This might be
the birthday of a discontinuous dance,
one that I weave
    from my low devout melancholie.
Where could I throw
the dice of my quarrel with a canon
who has offered me salvation?

Turn again
to the triple-tonguing bird.
Count it no evasion.
Count it the consolation for poets
uneasy with the assurance
    of a troubled breath.
Breathe now in celebration of blindness.
Breathe now for the intensional
resolution,
given to words forever in flight.

Legends lie on the water here.
The silver river wears a red veil.
One can rest assured of the olive trees

in Tuscany,
and of the borrowed magia
the Montevideo night tempers
into a different suffering,
all that is temporall,

all

that is imaginatively displaced.
It is enough to argue that these
are desire's accoutrements.
One among us will.

One among us will be mistaken.
You must feel
the edge of this threnody,
the exospheric probing that comes

as an accusation.
The silver river begins
its elliptical orbit about a poet's soul,
and a pilgrim's emptiness
must enter as grace,
or go deeper than the destination of the dead.

I am hymn deep in the harmony of my own
forgiveness.

I have given myself a promise:
there is an end to such judgment,
a modulation in the spirit
that even you, therapeutic,
could not deny me.

                        You turn,
and turn again,
following a fixed psalm,
anxious to confess your betrayal
                        of yourself.
I would make you that dying swan,
a voice with a proclamation of intent,
a body clothed with an irresolute need;
I would reward you
with the devastation of your muse's
                        white sincerity.
We have been at table with forgetfulness,
and have found it easy to pretend
that our stillness
            is a reconciliation
with the absence of desire.

                        Out of the wood of Buenos Aires,
the blind singer arrives,

spinning harmoniously with his bullroarer,
cocksure of his innocence.

        Time now
for the counterpoint of solitude,
the deftly displaced
        plagal cadence
that structures the plainsong
           of a disruptive
              choir.

So the three of us,
are four,
or two,
or one,
naughty with the spices of infinity
at heart,
durable, with the elixir of uncertainty,
too cozy with love's momentary flare.

I lift this turbulent spirit
into the morning air,
and release the temperate iron

bird within me.

That

is a provocative misapprehension,

dissembling stroke of a clock,

or a cock,

the unnatural configuration of knees

at prayer,

the lunar phase of a rekindled planet,

arguments with wind that leaves

its smudgy fingerprints upon a wall.

Who is in this house?

And where has invention gone?

Who cloisters the dense plasma

in the sun's corona?

Something perhaps sacred will erase

all evidence of ambition.

Velvet Granada.

The unbidden horse of Andalucía.

How will you constrain me?

My face to the wall,

I awaken to the ash of an old cemetery.

The bell I have used

                to gather my attention

speaks a language I would hide from you.

Dream of the Assyrian dog asleep on the Po.

Leave me to barter with the king

              who has abandoned me.

Soul moves on,

will not insist upon the sanctified

embrace, the clairvoyant eye,

nor the breathing confederacy

of this critical choir,

              nor the crucial

grace harrowing its way

              into the room.

This is the history of falling breath,

the claim of mothers who never appear.

I sit in the fervor of annihilation,

on the threshold of a moment

that would seed me my own dimension.

I would begin again.

I would search the scalar quantity

              of an arrested body.

My being grows shabby,
searching a thermal equilibrium.
What of austerity could I bring to you,
my choir and didaskaloi?
What,
in the evasive history of my holiness,
would enchant you?
I have pressed the light from this room,
and have suppressed the music.
I wait.

You see now:
a vermilion Eye of God
desert chicory
desert anemone
Apache plume
jojoba

"There is a fundamental contradiction
between observational conditions
and definitional possibilities";
a ritual complementarity

                    shadows our exchange.
Only here
can this rekindled silence
measure
            one and one,
and over again,
            to reach the limits of my craft,
the ambiguous shape of a fugitive force.

            You see now:
            kuduo
            aggrey beads
            Akua ba
            Ibeji
            a Kanaga mask

The archaeology of joy
guides me through the darkest
edge of emptiness,
                this space
that is no space.
I submit myself

to the rationality of weightlessness,
to the perfect history of contingency.
A thread of dust,
        light's surrogate,
finds me already at rest upon my stool,
or gathered in my own becoming
           upon that stool.
Perhaps the body knows
the probable curve of its own act,
an end I will not seek.
           I come close
to my heron intuition,
to the descriptive presence of my own doubt,
its indecipherable shape and configuration.
          What belongs to midnight?
I propose a pragmatic
sunset,
      magnetic fields holding clouds
collapsing under their own weight.
So I will write these things
     as form and rule,
        a disruptive

settling into the body's knowledge.
Such pride encourages
the ibis-headed god to weigh my heart.
And my atomistic unfaithfulness
                speaks clearly
                to the love
                that has no end.

Say that our old fires are now extinguished.
I detect an ancient piety:
                sprouts
                wheat sprout pudding
                apple
                lotus
                garlic
                sumac
                vinegar

I am at birth upon my own birth,
incarnate,
expedient,
discreet,

devoted to a prehensive will,

living an unbreakable order,

dispensable,

inescapable,

a ruby-throated hummingbird

who finds the sun and water enough

              in the cloistered hyssop.

I feel the distraction of wind chimes

on a desert floor.

             Pebbles chime

deep in a mountain stream.

I do not hear these things.

There are footsteps at the base of my skull.

I do not hear these things.

A robin constructs a waltz in its lilac nest.

Ear or eye, I find my engagement devious,

and the sly mismanagement of summer

a dutiful, ambiguous gift.

Just so, I find myself

at work on a geography of birds.

I should elicit the triangular
capacities of turtledove and grouse
and doṅu bird,
             something
to disorient wintry Hölderlin,
imprisoned in an Athenian rise and fall.

¡O ritmo de semillas secas!
That would stir the salutary
orientation of a crystal rug,
a kente cloth and a dancing kilt.
             By whose command?
It is too early to address
the blue field of a god's ambition.
"Water sleeps for an hour."
             I walk away
from my own shaping breath.

Where is the virtue
if the atom walks away from its power?
I have often sat
in the affective troposphere of Jemez,

and have awaited the disfiguring
order of a perfect solitude.
I move now upon this horizon,
as fertile as any mother,
                following
the radical movement of the canyon
light,
dancing at ease in my double estate.
This, I know,
is motion without a cause,
a substantive dance without measure,
                or the possibility of measure.
That crescent light is my spine,
as empty as the mask I wear
                upon my mind.
Speak to me of the rain's
consonant configuration,
        of the intervallic play of a voice
        speaking in prayer,
        or singing in devastation.
These matters arise in islands
where death has set its face against

its own imperfection.

These matters arise

where love disguises its perfection.

Who has taught me

the theology of the boiled fruit of the Dano tree,

the crushed Bana rock,

these powdered cattle bones,

the brilliant gold of clay?

Who has taught me

the sustaining music in a body's

fall from grace?

So the body will sound,

unlike the dutiful string,

within its own frequency,

and thereby disarm the continuity

we thought our bravest possession.

"What, if I do this,

will happen?"

Words that compel

a transformative intent, or words

that begin the demise of Being.

Siempre he dicho que yo iría a Santiago/
en un coche de agua negra.

(Three matadores, dressed in their trajes de luces, approach in single file. A trumpet announces the corrida's paseo. The matadores stop, remove their capotes de paseo and take up their capotes. They begin the unfurling ritual.)

> *I do not hear the clock*
> *at the far end of the room,*
> *nor the bell that brought me*
> *to this seat.*

(The matadores salute an invisible audience. M_1 turns to M_2.)

M_1: Comenciste avec une faute.

M_2: ¡No me jodas!

M_3: Speak in a language we understand.

(M_2 spins in a farol. M_1 and M_3 execute a series of passes.)

> *I am suddenly*
> *a gossamer thread,*
> *lifted from within,*
> *sheared from this moment,*
> *a process given substance*
> *by a trinity*
> *who will not speak to me.*

(M_3 folds his capote, and offers to embrace M_2.)

M_3: Ven.

(They embrace. M_1 offers to embrace M_2.)

M_1: Ven.

(They embrace.)

M_3: That was handled in good fashion.

M_2: Characteristically.

M_1: Impeccably.

M_3: It was only a beginning. Attend to the music.

They want us to shine.

M_2: Or to die.

M_1: ¡Basta!

M_2: That labyrinth we passed, these lengthening
shadows have taught me to fear.

M_3: We do not discuss such matters.

M_1: Blood is my star.

¡Cuidense con mis banderilleros!

M_3: (to M_2) You and I will be silent here in the shadows.
Prepared.

M_2: Certainly.

M_1: Why damn me with that alluring arrow:
suerte?

M_2: I meant to take it up with you.

M₃: Not now.

> *I started on the wrong foot.*
>
> *I passed in the wrong way.*
>
> *The robe was a darkness*
>
> *that blinded me.*

(M₁ takes his muleta, pivots, raising his montera to the invisible audience, tosses his montera, and steps decisively toward the center of the arena.)

M₃: Here, let them close their eyes.

> We will not show this.

M₂: Exactly.

M₁: (turning) Who are you to deny me this opportunity?

M₃: It was a momentary decision,

> I assure you.

M₂: There was no conspiracy. After all,

> we are all involved.

M₁: Not until I lead.

M₃: Lead, lead.

> Who goes first?
>
> Napoleon goes first.

M₁: Spitefulness. Envy.

M₃: Not at all.

Cuando la paloma quiere ser

cigueña.

M₂: How he preens himself.

The Andalusi delivered from Hebrew appurtenances.

M₁: Deliver me from this idiot.

M₃: You dedicated your faena to a fiction.

Do you think we can forgive you?

Can I be forgiven

for being unprepared

to address the small

bead of submission

within me?

(M₁ begins a series of passes with his muleta.)

M₂: Why not stand in one place?

M₃: Catch your breath?

M₂: Think about your carelessness?

M₃: About your impurity?

Can I be forgiven

for going beyond

the evidence of my return

to here,

a place from which

I have never set out?

M$_1$: Badly stated, that

Verbum dicendi.

Acceptance.

Word for the sake of form.

M$_3$: Whatever you say,

whatever you do,

it remains sacred,

this space that is no space,

this space we carry with us

from air to air.

M$_2$: Though compromised in Sevilla.

M$_3$: Impugned in Lima.

M$_1$: Redeemed, perhaps, in Madrid.

M$_3$: Never fulfilled in Caracas.

M$_2$: El apoderado nos mandan a Puebla.

M$_1$: With images of Salamanca.

M$_3$: And the bracing exigencies of Barcelona.

M$_2$: Our desire is a map of failure.

M$_1$: I trust you to keep that to yourself.

M$_2$: Velvet Granada.

M$_1$: Where did you hear that?

M$_3$: Come here now.

Let's arrange ourselves.

M_1: For?

M_3: For the momentary dance we three can do
without a home.

(They gather. Aligned, M_1, M_2, M_3. Then M_2, M_3, M_1. Shift to
M_2, M_1, M_3. Then M_3, M_1, M_2. Then M_1, M_3, M_2. To M_3, M_2, M_1.
Then M_2, M_3, M_1. Finally M_1, M_2, M_3. They begin a litany of
cities.)

M_1, M_2, M_3: Jerez

Córdoba

Burgos

Pamplona

Guadalajara

Monterrey

Bilbao

San Sebastián

M_1: I sense an urgent misapprehension.

M_2: A miscalculation.

M_3: Sit still.

And weep.

Sit still

under the laceration

of all your faults,

under the heavy

water of all your

misgivings.

The danger lies

in being softly bundled

into mindlessness.

M_3: Where is the trumpet?

Let it sound now

to rescue us.

(M_1 starts to execute a series of passes.)

Too late.

It is too late for that.

The art is gone.

M_2: But they want us to shine?

M_3: They?

Who are they?

Nothing but memory now,

the legacy of some prior disturbance.

But that equation never serves.

Someone is trying to phrase the sparrow's lament,

a fortspinnung that will embody

a river and the feathery

appearance of my own birth,
that deceptive cadence sounding
a bone's breadth and dimension.
How cleverly I close my hands
upon that primordial moment,
uneasy with the way the light in this room
shades my other body.
Where is the flame?
Such weary light folds upon itself,
searching the breach in my adobe wall,
the negotiation of sunless stones upon the path.
My teacher insists that another star
would be more assertive,
more careful of its progress
through the tempered
and tempering air,
and would leap past the resistant
endowment of death.
Say that my mind claims the journey as its own;
say that my spirit has learned to live
on the other side of desire.
Imagine now

the quantum superposition of desire,
and a body at rest,
moving with magnetic force
      aslant of every desire.
These things we do not record.

A second bell sounds.
Perhaps I feel it sound, and think,
here is something familiar,
though I know it was struck
      thousands of years
        before I approached this room.

Oh, bright algebraist,
I know how inexact my spirit
has become,
too satisfied with probabilities,
with measurements flowing out of a past
my body could not have known,
too eager for finished calculations
that leave an unanswered question.

So I sit here,
jealous of a constancy that runs
                    away from me.
I struck the second bell.
I brought this world into being.
I am persuaded I have written
        the perfect epitaph to advance my fame.
But the hole remains scaled;
the light asks for a decision
at the moment of a masked impulse.

Trust this eye to know
the form of that maple the window reveals.
Trust the flesh to feel
the aged wind in that rising bird call.
We need not set our need under erasure.
I have awakened,
        to exile
        all virtue
        from this domain.
I must master again
a threshold ingenuity, conjure

a goat path that leads
      to a naming and a burial.

My exponential galaxy remains
an engulfing silence, an axiomatic
entanglement beyond my touch.
      I follow the meridian now,
      from hip bone to foot.
      It is Sunday,
      the first of August,
      and white and black and red.
      It is a bull,
      lying in its purple blood
      in a sunless arena.
      It is a clabbered parchment,
      freed from the tree roots
      that have hidden it.
Breathe
with the stone falcon set at the door.
Begin
the excision of dreams,
the perturbation of the scandalous

ecstasy I have constructed of disregard
and neglect.
So much as this poor song testifies—
Let me sleep.
A spiraling figure
tests this cloistered air.
I would ask its name, but know
I would be in error.
Oh, but I savor my miscalculations
and the arbitrary edge they give
my inventiveness.
Green moments and scarlet interludes
make me unfaithful to the sudden
hummingbird.
I have set myself to solve the ceasing
instant, the leaping exactitude
of a migrating star.
Es colibrí de la izquierda,
without a voice,
without my insecurity
in the face of a tactless eye.

I could offer my life on a divining tray,
and follow the spiraling logic that keeps me
returning to the fossil record of a soul
        I explore in reverential anger.

Who has taught me this?
What voice have I borrowed
        to express a necessary silence?

What do you bring to the door?
    A tattered Lachesian shawl
    the shattered lid of a clay pot
    a hemispheric map of a cat's brain

The Egyptian tells me
I am at home,
a bride of my own being.
I know myself a creature formed
by the fading presence of shape
shifting cities,
        an elemental trace,
given depth and dimension

by the contradiction she displays.
I would construct a canopy of proof,
a bone dense argument for my presence,
some coursing intensity
                    as flexible as water.
I pretend
that I will go deep, and deeper,
into the frangible beneficence
        of the instructed eye,
following the bright bedrock of doubt,
the uplifted innocence of exhilaration.
He derretido mi alma
in a misplaced passion for pity,
and the mathematical inversion
                    of desire.
Should I now reason
        with evasion?
Should I now address that oak
beyond the window,
and reason that the accident
of arboreal life will someday seize
its roots—make it subject

to infestation, gaseous injury,
or a rude cut that never heals?
Should I now seize upon these words
as my own,
an investment
in the fertile notion of death within me?

Nothing transfigures
the resurrections that "waken mee."
I place myself near the breath-devouring
substance of absent bodies;
perhaps that "fundamental speck
of negative energy"
awakens a tremor in me.
These moments will always disturb.
Ancient of days,
the mathematikoi draw near
to their task, and retreat,
the fundamental speck resisting
its containment.
Should I sit in this choir,
an adept at a tuneful constellation,

lending my voice to a form
            that moves beyond itself?
suffer again that mittelalter lie,
the wood's transitive possession?
I am not so beguiled
by the flowering electron
            as by the flowing physical intuition
            that places me here.
I shall walk carefully
about this contradiction—
            the changed dimension
that marks my native speech,
the salutary inscription that settles
                            my bones.
You perhaps would reward me
with a necessary darkness
            to complete my silence,
            to calculate my stillness,
            to tally the accidental light
            that explodes and escapes,
                        and figures me.
We have, you and I, enough silk

for the forest's disarmed, disarming, body;
enough of familiar flannel for the desert's
plunge into coldness;
enough of a damask rose
              to enfold a city; all
the imaginative delights of an assimilation
we can never trace.
Who is the betrayed one,
if my body sits motionless and here
gives in, as my mind tolls its dissolution?
What finer thoroughfare for the spirit
than an uncharted path,
        or a path that has been transformed
        by leading nowhere?
So, if the morning arrives
in an amethyst coach bearing sacred garments,
all is the relevant case of related moments,
touching and falling apart,
reconfigured in the alchemy of a spirit
              that would annihilate itself.
Abruptly,
time conjures its demise.

We arise, you and I,
such fleeting and fearful akusmatoí,
entangled by the breath
          the morning counts within us.

Through a moment of infinite density,
I recognize a radiant corruption
that serves as a cradle
          for my emptiness.
I have become attuned
to the disappearance of all things
and of my self,
and to that "purely present content"
that nurtures the "sheer fact of being."

Here begins the revelation of a kiosk
beside the road: the white eggs
nestled there in straw
turn blue in the amber light.
Make of that what you will,
say, what you desire,
a pilgrimage

a secular mourning,
a morning given over to meditation.
This is the place set aside
for creating the body,
a source of fluctuations, unmarked
by singularity.
Call this wandering along this road
a colonization.

SELECTED DALKEY ARCHIVE PAPERBACKS

SELECTED DALKEY ARCHIVE PAPERBACKS

FOR A FULL LIST OF PUBLICATIONS, VISIT: WWW.DALKEYARCHIVE.COM